The Ethi
Environmental Management

Does Stewardship Lead Us Down a Blind Alley?

Martin J Hodson
Principal Tutor, Christian Rural and Environmental Studies (CRES)

Margot R Hodson
Director of Theology and Education, The John Ray Initiative

GROVE BOOKS LIMITED
RIDLEY HALL RD CAMBRIDGE CB3 9HU

Contents

Acknowledgments

We thank the Grove Ethics Group for giving us this opportunity, and especially Tim Howles and Guido de Graaff who gave us great editorial support.

First Impression October 2024

ISSN 1470-854X

ISBN 978 1 78827 419 7

Introduction

1

> The Lord God took the man and put him in the Garden of Eden to work it and take care of it. (Gen 2.15 NIV)

Since the dawn of agriculture humanity has been engaged in managing the environment. The biblical narrative suggests that we should 'work it and take care of it' (or 'tend and keep' in the King James Version). The Bible has much practical advice on land management, particularly in the Old Testament, for example: Sabbath; sabbatical year; jubilee; and gleaning. These concepts undergird the biblical stewardship ethic. At the time they were written, the global human population was around 170 million, we had not discovered how to use fossil fuels, and our impact on the planet was relatively small. However, that has changed, and there are now 8.1 billion people on the earth (in 2024), with the pressures on the environment that brings (such as deforestation, habitat loss). Moreover, since the Industrial Revolution we have been burning fossil fuels at an increasing rate leading to an increase in atmospheric carbon dioxide concentration. That, together with other greenhouse gas emissions (*eg* methane, nitrous oxide) has caused an increase in global temperature of about 1.2°C above the pre-industrial temperature by 2024. We have not been good at 'tending and keeping,' and the need to improve our methodologies for environmental management is now urgent. This booklet will explore current trends in environmental management and their ethical foundations. We will ask whether stewardship is a suitable ethic to undergird environmental management or has it been part of the problem? Are there other approaches and are these best used independently or in combination with a stewardship approach?

Before we consider environmental management it is important that we delineate the extent of the problem. As we write in 2024, we not infrequently hear people talking of an environmental crisis, but what are the main issues facing us? One way of categorizing the environmental issues is to outline the planetary boundaries concept. First proposed by Johan Rockström and his colleagues in 2009, it sought to determine 'a safe operating space for humanity.'[1] This is a very anthropocentric aim, but that kind of thinking is common in this area. Rockström *et al* proposed nine boundaries, seven of which they had enough data to assess, three of which were already crossed: biosphere integrity (including biodiversity loss); climate change; and biogeochemical flows (the phosphorus and nitrogen cycles). The planetary boundaries were updated by Will Steffen and colleagues in 2015,[2] and then again by Katherine Richardson and colleagues in 2023.[3] By 2023, the scientists had enough data to assess all nine boundaries. As had been determined before, the boundaries for biosphere integrity, climate change and biogeochemical flows were exceeded, but it was now recognized that land-system change, freshwater change, and novel entities (which includes plastic and chemical pollution) were also over the limits. Stratospheric ozone depletion, atmospheric aerosol loading and ocean acidification have yet to exceed their boundaries, but the latter is now close to doing so.

Humanity has pushed the planet over six boundaries, and that level of dominance and damage means we are now in the era of the Anthropocene. This is defined by the Oxford Dictionary as 'the current geological age, viewed as the period during which human activity has been the dominant influence on climate and the environment.'[4] The Anthropocene has been a controversial concept, not because of the reality of its existence but through difficulties of defining a start date for the era.[5] The state of the global environment is not at all good, and this threatens the continued existence of humanity and much of the world's biodiversity on this planet. We have not been successful so far in managing the environment, and many fear that if we do not improve it will lead to disaster.

The state of the global environment threatens the continued existence of humanity

In this booklet we will begin by laying out some of the basic concepts behind environmental management approaches: preservation, conservation and sustainability. We will then move on to consider how humanity has attempted to manage the global environment, particularly since the Rio Earth Summit took place in 1992. It is clear that many of the world's environmental problems can be attributed to our prevailing economic model, and the following section will look at how we can manage both money and the environment in a sustainable way. Finally, where does ethics come into all of this? If you ask the average member of a church congregation for their thoughts on how we should look after the environment they will almost certainly mention the word 'stewardship.' But whilst the idea of stewardship is still widely used at the local church level, it has come under various attacks from ethicists and theologians in recent years. In our final two chapters we will examine these issues and seek a way forward.

Preservation, Conservation and Sustainability

2

> The words preservation and conservation are often used interchangeably, but the two concepts are quite different. Conservation protects the environment through the responsible use of natural resources. Preservation protects the environment from harmful human activities.[6]

Before we embark on our survey of environmental management it is important that we look briefly at some of the key concepts that underlie this topic, and that we set these in historical context. More information on this subject can be found in our previous Grove booklet, *An Introduction to Environmental Ethics*.[7] Here we will consider preservation and conservation before moving on to sustainability.

In its extreme versions, *preservation* means that an area of land is totally cordoned off, such that humans are prevented from entry. The idea can be traced back to the American transcendentalists, Henry David Thoreau and Ralph Waldo Emerson, and particularly to John Muir, who was very influenced by them.[8] Muir was greatly attracted to wilderness and spent much of his time trekking in Canadian and American forests and mountainous areas. In his early days he was very committed to the complete protection of wilderness, but he became somewhat more pragmatic when negotiating the establishment of the Yosemite National Park in California.

Muir was an idealist, seeing the preservation of wilderness as a laudable aim that would protect the land from development, free from the influence of humanity. However, there was one major problem with this thinking, and that was the presence of indigenous people on the land that was designated for preservation. Often these people had lived on the land for millennia, and were very much part of the ecology, managing the land in a sustainable way. In the case of Yosemite, the Ahwahnechee band of Miwok people were slowly expelled from their land after its designation as a national park.[9] Unfortunately, the idea of setting up pristine wilderness reserves spread from the United States around the world, and it often fitted the colonialist thinking of the time. One might think that this fortress conservation approach would have died out by now, but this is very far from the case. As Fletcher *et al* state, 'Despite decades of critical engagement by Indigenous and non-Indigenous observers, large international nongovernmental organizations, philanthropists, global institutions, and nation-states continue to uphold the notion of pristine landscapes as wilderness in conservation ideals and practices.'[10] The recent United Nations' idea that we should set aside 30% of the planet for nature has drawn some criticism from indigenous groups who fear that this will lead to them being removed from their land.[11]

Conservation is a difficult word to define, but in the context of nature conservation the Oxford English Dictionary describes it as 'the preservation, protection, or restoration of the natural environment and of wildlife.' Among the early conservationists George Perkins Marsh stands out, warning that, 'Man is everywhere a disturbing agent. Wherever he plants his foot, the harmonies of nature are turned to discords.'[12] Writing in the 1860s he was quite prophetic in forecasting the environmental problems that humanity would face if it did not manage resources wisely. Unlike the preservationists who wanted to withdraw from wilderness areas, conservationists like Marsh wanted to manage them. Following on from Marsh were Gifford Pinchot and Aldo Leopold, who established the foundations of the environmental movement and were definitely interventionist in their approaches. Leopold was a forester whose *A Sand County Almanac*, published posthumously, became a classic.[13] It was there that he proposed the land ethic, suggesting that land should not be seen solely in economic terms.[14]

As we entered the second half of the twentieth century it became increasingly obvious that environmental issues were becoming more important, and were now of global scope. Rachel Carson's *Silent Spring* (1962) reported that residues from insecticides could be detected thousands of miles from where they were used.[15] If pollutants were now spreading globally, then there needed to be responses from international bodies like the United Nations. Moreover, it was increasingly recognized that environment and world development needed to be considered together. The first Earth Day was held on 22 April 1970. From the 1970s there were a number of key publications and reports including: Paul Ehrlich's *The Population Bomb* (1970); Barry Commoner's *The Closing Circle* (1971); *A Blueprint for Survival* (1972); *The Limits to Growth* (1972); René Dubos' and Barbara Ward's *Only One Earth: The Care and Maintenance of a Small Planet* (1972); E F Schumacher's *Small is Beautiful* (1973); and Herman Daly's *The Sustainable Society* (1977).[16] The latter publication focused on the topic of *sustainability*, somewhat before the World Commission on Environment and Development under the leadership of Norwegian Prime Minister, Gro Harlem Brundtland, began its work. Their report, *Our Common Future* (1987), gave us the well-known definition of sustainable development: 'development that meets the needs of the present without compromising the ability of future generations to meet their own needs.'[17]

Management at an International Level

3

> Perhaps the most important common ground we must arrive at in Rio is the understanding that we are all in this together. No place on the planet can remain an island of affluence in a sea of misery. We're either going to save the whole world or no-one will be saved. (Maurice F Strong)[18]

The Rio Conference

Our Common Future (1987) concluded with a call to action which directly led to the United Nations Conference on Environment and Development, held in Rio de Janeiro, Brazil (3–14 June 1992).[19] The Rio Conference, also known as the Earth Summit, was crucial in many respects. There global environmental issues gained the attention of world leaders and governments for the first time, or at least it has been perceived that way. A total of 27 principles were agreed, some of which have guided future legislation and practice, including:[20]

Principle 2 accepts 'the responsibility (of states) to ensure that activities within their jurisdiction or control do not cause damage to the environment of other states or of areas beyond the limits of national jurisdiction.' This was an acknowledgment that pollution was now transboundary and global in nature.

Principle 16 accepts 'that the polluter should, in principle, bear the cost of pollution.' This 'polluter pays principle' has been widely adopted in legislation on areas as diverse as contaminated land and global climate policy. Often the problem in implementing it is deciding who precisely the polluter is (or was).

Principle 17 stated that 'environmental impact assessment, as a national instrument, shall be undertaken for proposed activities that are likely to have a significant adverse impact on the environment.' This led to many nations enshrining environmental impact assessments (EIA) in their planning and development laws. Whenever a major development is proposed an EIA is required to consider likely effects and suggest possible mitigation actions.[21]

Two other documents were produced for the Rio Conference: Forest Principles and Agenda 21. Forest Principles was a non-legally binding agreement which made some recommendations for forest conservation and management. Of greater importance, Agenda 21 was the main attempt by the Rio Conference to look at sustainable development.[22] It was part of the thinking that eventually led on to the Millennium Development Goals (MDGs) and the Sustainable Development Goals (SDGs) that we will discuss below. The Rio Conference also established three legally-binding conventions: the United Nations Framework Convention on Climate Change (UNFCCC); the Convention on Biological Diversity (CBD); and the UN Convention to Combat Desertification (UNCCD). By far the least well known, the UNCCD entered into force in December 1996, and established a series of annual Conference of the Parties (COP) meetings, essentially the signatory countries to the convention, but these became biennial in 2001. The work of the CBD, and especially that of the UNFCCC, is much better known, and will be considered below.

Managing the Atmosphere and the Climate

Before moving on to climate change it is important briefly to mention two other issues concerning the atmosphere: acid rain and ozone depletion. Sulphur dioxide pollution, caused by the burning of coal that was high in sulphur content, was the principal cause of acid rain. In the atmosphere, sulphur dioxide reacted with water to produce sulphuric acid, which then eventually returned to the ground as acidic precipitation. In the 1970s and 1980s large parts of Europe and North America were badly impacted, with forest dieback and lake acidification becoming major problems. In 1979, 32 countries including Canada, the United States and many European countries signed the United Nations Economic Commission for Europe (UNECE) Convention on Long-range Transboundary Air Pollution.[23] This instructed signatory governments to introduce legislation on installing scrubbers to remove sulphur dioxide from the flue gases at power stations. As a result, acid rain was markedly reduced, and the problem, if not totally solved, is at least under better control.

Ozone depletion began to be noticed in the 1970s. This was mainly caused by chlorofluorocarbons (CFCs), often used as refrigerants, which, when released, broke down ozone in the upper atmosphere. This is of major concern as ozone forms a screen preventing some ultraviolet radiation reaching the ground. Famously, an ozone hole formed over the Antarctic. Again, the United Nations took swift action, and the Montreal Protocol was agreed in 1987.[24] Production of CFCs was severely restricted, and ozone depletion was markedly reduced. It is notable that in these two instances, acid rain and ozone depletion, prompt international action was taken, which significantly decreased the problems. Sadly, climate change has proven much more complex to deal with.

The Intergovernmental Panel on Climate Change (IPCC) is the United Nations body that is charged with keeping the world up to date on the latest climate science.[25] Founded in 1988, it has now produced six assessment reports, and in the first part of the sixth assessment, published in 2021, it pronounced that the climate crisis was 'unequivocally' caused by human activities.[26] Although the IPCC does not take policy decisions concerning the management of the climate, it does inform those decisions.

The United Nations Framework Convention on Climate Change (UNFCCC)[27] published five principles, two of which have been particularly important in guiding future work and negotiations:[28]

Principle 1 states that 'the Parties should protect the climate system for the benefit of present and future generations of humankind, on the basis of equity and in accordance with their common but differentiated responsibilities and respective capabilities.' This looks to future generations, but again shows a clear anthropocentric bias. The principle is notable for its statement on 'common but differentiated responsibilities,' which implied that rich countries might be expected to pay more to solve the problems of climate change. This has been one of the major sticking points in climate negotiations for many years.

Principle 3 stipulates that 'Parties should take precautionary measures to anticipate, prevent or minimize the causes of climate change and mitigate its adverse effects. Where there are threats of serious or irreversible damage, lack of full scientific certainty should not be used as a reason for postponing such measures...' This precautionary principle was later applied much wider than climate change, but became quite a controversial concept in some quarters. The problem with much work on climate change is that the results are expressed in terms of probabilities. So, for example, at some stage there might be a 95–99% probability that an aspect of climate change was caused by humans, but this implies that there is a 1–5% probability it was not. This apparent uncertainty was seized upon by many climate sceptics, who used it as a pretext not to take action on global warming.[29]

As with UNCCD, annual Conference of the Parties (COP) meetings were set up under the auspices of the UNFCCC. The first United Nations Climate Change Conference (COP1) was held in Berlin in 1995. In 1997, COP3 met in Kyoto, Japan and agreed to reduce greenhouse gas emissions by 6–8%, relative to a 1990 benchmark, by 2012 (the Kyoto Protocol). This then required ratification by each government. The process took until November 2004 when Russia eventually signed and the Protocol entered force on 16 February 2005. The United States is the one country that never ratified the Protocol. Al Gore signed the agreement as Vice President, but the US congress would not ratify it. The next administration, under President George W Bush, explicitly rejected the Protocol, with Bush writing in 2001, 'As you know, I oppose the Kyoto Protocol because it exempts 80 percent of the world, including major population centres such as China and India, from compliance, and would cause serious harm to the US economy.'[30] The Kyoto Protocol was originally intended to end in 2012, and by COP15 in Copenhagen in 2009 it was evident that a further agreement would be needed. COP15 was a great disappointment to many people, and no legally-binding agreement on carbon emissions cuts was made. The one significant announcement that was made was that global temperature rise was to be limited to no more than 2°C above the pre-industrial temperature. The Kyoto Protocol was eventually extended until 2020, and the Paris Agreement of 2015 ultimately replaced it.

For COP21 in Paris in 2015 a different approach was used. Christiana Figueres was Executive Secretary of UNFCCC at the time, and she decided to ask governments for carbon emissions reduction commitments known as 'Intended Nationally Determined Contributions' or INDCs. The UN then added up these commitments to give a global picture. The promised cuts were not enough to reach the 2°C target, but COP21 introduced a ratcheting process, whereby governments would be frequently asked for new INDCs with the hope that they would gradually become more ambitious. One surprise was that some low-lying nations, concerned that sea level rise would overrun them, asked for a 1.5°C target. They were successful, and the final text suggested that the target should be 'well below 2°C' and that we should 'pursue efforts to limit' the rise even more to meet a target of 1.5°C.[31]

The UNFCCC process has continued since COP21, but it has become increasingly obvious that emissions cuts are not happening fast enough. There has been some progress in other areas, and at COP27 in Egypt in 2022 a historic 'Loss and Damage' agreement was signed.[32] The intention here was that rich countries, who have historically been the biggest carbon emitters, should pay for the damage this has caused to poor nations. As with all such schemes, the main difficulty is in persuading the rich countries to pay their share.

Much of the work of the UNFCCC, documented above, has concerned efforts to cut carbon emissions, and thereby reduce anthropogenic climate change. They also recognize the importance of adaptation, and indeed the IPCC has a whole section of its reports dedicated to that topic. Increasingly, it is acknowledged that carbon emissions cuts are not happening quickly enough to decrease warming, and that adaptation efforts may not be enough to cope with future climate change. What other possibilities are there? Essentially there are two: carbon dioxide removal (CDR) and solar radiation modification (SRM).[33] With CDR the proposal is to remove carbon dioxide that is already present in the atmosphere, with the intention of decreasing its warming effect. At its simplest, this can involve planting trees or increasing carbon sequestration in the soil. Considerable research is taking place into direct air capture machines that will suck carbon dioxide out of the atmosphere, and then store it safely, but at present these are expensive technologies. There is also the idea of fertilizing parts of the ocean to increase the growth of algae that absorb carbon dioxide from the atmosphere. This is a controversial technology, as there are worries about potential side-effects. SRM technologies are all highly debateable, and involve reflecting solar radiation back into outer space. The most futuristic plans concern giant mirrors sent into orbit around the planet. However, the methodology that has gained most interest is stratospheric aerosol injection. Essentially, this involves mimicking the cooling effect of sulphate aerosols that are put into the atmosphere during volcanic eruptions. Again, side-effects are a concern (*eg* acid rain), but also what happens when the injections are stopped? Not surprisingly, there are considerable ethical implications of both CDR and SRM technologies that are beyond the scope of this booklet.[34]

Managing the Living World

The Convention on Biological Diversity (CBD) entered into force on 29 December 1993.[35] It has three aims: 'the conservation of biological diversity; the sustainable use of the components of biological diversity; and the fair and equitable sharing of the benefits arising out of the utilization of genetic resources.' In contrast to the climate change COPs, the biodiversity COPs organized under the CBD have gained far less public attention. COP1 was held in Nassau in the Bahamas in 1994. Since then, they have usually been held every two years. COP10, held in Nagoya, Japan, in 2010 was particularly significant as it led to both the Nagoya Protocol on Access to Genetic Resources, and to the 'Strategic Plan for Biodiversity, 2011–2020.' This was succeeded by the Kunming-Montreal Global Biodiversity Framework (GBF), an outcome of COP15 that was disrupted by the COVID-19 pandemic, and was held partly online and partly in person between 2021 and 2023. The Millennium Ecosystem Assessment (MA) was an initiative started in 2000 at the suggestion of Kofi Annan, the United Nations Secretary-General at the time.[36] The MA received over $14 million in grants, principally from the UN. It completed its work in 2005, producing a number of reports documenting the state of biodiversity at that time and enunciating a number of key principles. The MA was a major promoter of the ecosystem services concept, and they defined this as 'the benefits people obtain from ecosystems.' Ecosystem services are divided into four categories: provisioning, regulating, cultural and supporting services. Provisioning services include food, water, fibres and fuel, while regulating services embrace climate, flood and disease regulation and water purification. Cultural services include aesthetic, spiritual, educational and recreational aspects. Finally, supporting services involve nutrient cycling, soil formation, primary production (*eg* photosynthesis) and other processes that are not directly used by people. The MA was undoubtedly driven primarily by political economy concerns and by anthropocentric ethics, but it did at least recognize that a broader ethical framing would be necessary to protect biodiversity: 'ultimately, the level of biodiversity that survives on earth will be determined not just by utilitarian considerations but to a significant extent by ethical concerns, including considerations of the intrinsic values of species.'[37] Despite the activity outlined above, biodiversity has continued to fall, and in 2022 WWF found that the relative abundance of monitored wildlife populations showed a 69% decrease between 1970 and 2018.[38]

Managing Sustainable Development

Throughout the 1990s there was increasing unease about world development, and particularly the alleviation of poverty. Concern for development and concern for the environment were often seen as separate and even competing issues. This perception has gradually decreased during the twenty-first century, most particularly as climate change has been seen to impact poor people the most. The UN-sponsored Millennium Summit in 2000 eventually led to the stating of the Millennium Development Goals (MDGs) in 2001.[39] There were eight goals, only one of which ('Goal 7: ensure environmental sustainability') specifically concerned the environment. The MDGs were intended to run until 2015, and as they were ending several assessments were made concerning their success. In many areas, including the eradication of poverty, good progress had been made. But Goal 7 was well off target with both biodiversity loss and the impacts of climate change increasing. It was feared that the progress made on alleviating poverty could be reversed if environmental degradation was not addressed. When it came to replacing the MDGs with the Sustainable Development Goals (SDGs) in 2015, it was recognized that greater emphasis would be needed to be placed on the environment. Of the 17 SDGs, seven have some environmental focus.[40] Sadly, the COVID-19 pandemic had a serious impact on progress in many areas, and in 2024 it was reported that only 17% of the SDGs were on track to be achieved by 2030 (when they are due to end).[41]

An Overarching Problem

As we have seen, despite the effort outlined above, the global environment continues to decline. There have been some successes with sustainable development, but these are under threat from climate change and environmental degradation. Key problems have been the unwillingness of rich countries to fund schemes that benefit the poor, and of multinational companies to put environmental concerns above shareholder profits. At a more local scale, although EIAs are now routinely carried out for large developments, even when they discover rare habitats, plants or animals, economic or development concerns often overrule. A classic example of this has been the destruction of ancient woodlands that were on the route of HS2, the new north-south rail line under construction in the UK.[42] Money and economics have dominated this whole area, and it is to this topic that we turn next.

4

Valuing Nature

> The reason that scientists expect catastrophic damages from temperature increases that economists assert will only slightly reduce the rate of economic growth is that scientists know what they're talking about when it comes to climate change, but economists frankly haven't got a clue. (Steve Keen)[43]

The Current Economic Model and the Environment

Consider, for a moment, the example of acid rain that we mentioned above. A power station owner makes money by selling energy to the local grid. That energy comes from the burning of coal which is rich in sulphur. The sulphur dioxide produced is the cause of acid rain that falls on a forest hundreds or thousands of miles away from the power station, mixed with acid rain that is generated from other similar power stations maybe even in different countries. The acid rain causes trees to die and the owner of the forest loses much of their income as a result. The power station causes pollution that has economic impacts elsewhere, but it does not figure in the balance sheet that the owner checks each year. The pollution is what economists call an 'externality' which is defined as 'a situation where the actions of some firm or individual have consequences for someone else who has no say in the matter.'[44] In the case of acid rain, as we have seen, governments brought in legislation that forced power stations to install scrubbers to remove sulphur dioxide. However, the power stations are still releasing vast amounts of carbon dioxide into the atmosphere, an additional externality that legislation has yet to bring under full control.

Another area we need to consider is the interaction between economic growth and the environment.[45] The classical view is that economic growth, particularly increase in gross domestic product (GDP), is a good thing, and that it should not limited by environmental boundaries. Another assessment, one taken by Nobel Prize-winning economist, William Nordhaus, is that environmental limitations will cause a drag on economic growth. However, some economists and environmentalists view the problem as being much more serious, the resources of the planet as finite, and conclude that this must surely lead to a cap on growth. We have already mentioned the 1972 report *Limits to Growth*, which suggested that economic growth would be halted by 2100 if not before.[46] The authors saw five factors that would interact to cause this: population increase, agricultural production, non-renewable resource depletion, industrial output and pollution generation.

The final topic we will consider here is that of discounting the future.[47] Discounting concerns the relative worth of current *versus* future values. In relation to climate change it asks whether we should invest a large amount of money now to cut carbon emissions so that future generations will be protected. Alternatively, should we not worry too much at the moment, anticipating that with economic growth people will be richer in the future and therefore able to solve problems arising from climate change via new advanced technologies. In this respect the cost of carbon is crucial. Lord (Nicholas) Stern suggested that we should have a high carbon cost to discourage the use of fossil fuels, and that immediate action on climate change through emissions cuts was required. Nordhaus argued for a low carbon cost, gradually ramping this up over time. There are huge intergenerational justice issues here. Do people today need to pay to protect people of the future, who might be better off and not need protection? But if Stern is ignored and the impacts of climate change make people a lot poorer, then we have seriously let down future generations. In practice, over the last few years, it appears that the international community has largely followed the advice of Nordhaus.

Do people today need to pay to protect people of the future?

Monetization of the Environment

Aldo Leopold was well ahead of his time when he saw that most plants and animals and some environments were perceived as having no economic value.[48] In effect they are regarded as externalities. This can have highly negative consequences. The Ecosystem Services concept, outlined above, suggested that the environment should be valued mainly for its uses by humanity. So, could we give monetary value to the environment, and take away its status as an externality? In one case study, British environmentalist Tony Juniper describes mangrove forests in Thailand that were removed to make way for shrimp farms, which brought in $1.5 billion per year to the Thai economy.[49] However, when other factors were taken into account (*eg* decreased protection of the coast against tropical storms) it was estimated that it had led to a net loss of $262 million per year. The Economics of Ecosystems and Biodiversity (TEEB), a global research initiative, attempts to take this sort of thinking further. They state, 'The TEEB initiative seeks to draw attention to the invisibility of nature in the economic choices we make across the domains of international, national, and local policy-making, public administration, and business. TEEB sees this invisibility as a key driver of the ongoing depletion of ecosystems and biodiversity.'[50] TEEB is well aware of criticisms that they are financializing nature, but argues that ecosystem services are already being looked at in this way. Theologian Richard Bauckham is critical of TEEB and similar schemes, arguing that '...as creatures of God the creatures are literally priceless and we degrade them by setting a price on them.'[51] Bauckham argues passionately for the intrinsic value of nature, while TEEB, and indeed most conservation biologists, favour extrinsic value. Pragmatically, they would argue that if we do not put a monetary value on nature, then that value will be set at zero in a financially-orientated world.

Carbon is one component of the environment where financial value is already given. Two approaches have been used: 'cap and trade' and 'carbon pricing.' With the first companies are given allowances, and can emit carbon up to a limit. Once that cap is reached they either pay a penalty, or buy allowances from other companies that have not reached their own limits and have some to sell. With carbon pricing the price is set and a tax is imposed. As we saw above, there is a considerable controversy over the correct price for carbon. There are pluses and minuses of both systems, but in both cases we are paying for something once regarded as an externality.[52]

Rethinking Environmental Economics

Traditionally, economics took very little interest in the environment, and until very recently it was not possible to study environmental economics on most university economics courses. However, that has gradually been changing with both economists that we may regard as establishment figures, and those who might be thought of as radicals, weighing in on the environment. Let us consider five from across this spectrum.

Dr Mark Carney is a Canadian and was Governor of the Bank of England from 2013 to 2020. In 2020 he gave the Reith Lectures, the final one being entitled 'From Climate Crisis to Real Prosperity.'[53] Carney is in no doubt about the scale of the problem: 'We won't have a financial system if we don't have a planet.' He went on to say that the financial system was funding temperature increases of over 3°C. Carney is, however, positive about the future, and believes that net zero and the transition to a green economy is the greatest commercial opportunity of our time.

Sir Partha Dasgupta is an Indian-British economist who is an Emeritus Professor of Economics at the University of Cambridge. He was asked by the UK Treasury to produce a report on the economics of biodiversity, with the final report being published in 2021.[54] In it, Dasgupta was very clear that there is a biodiversity crisis, and that part of the problem is that humanity sees itself as separate from nature, not a part of it. He went on to say, 'to detach nature from economic reasoning is to imply that we consider ourselves to be external to nature. The fault is not in economics; it lies in the way we have chosen to practise it. Transformative change is possible—we and our descendants deserve nothing less.'

Lord Stern, who we have already mentioned, is a professor at the London School of Economics and Political Science. He was the author of the *Stern Review on the Economics of Climate Change* in 2006 which was commissioned by the UK government.[55] Stern strongly believed that climate change needed to be tackled very quickly and that it would be much more expensive to tackle if the world delayed. Following the publication of the review, Stern entered into a heated debate with Nordhaus over the cost of carbon to use.

Steve Keen is an Australian economist and a critic of neoclassical economics. His work is wide-ranging. As can be seen from the quotation taken from his recent (2024) work at the head of this chapter, he is not very complimentary about the way some of his fellow economists think about climate change. Like Stern, Keen is particularly critical of Nordhaus, and does not mince his words: 'In fact, in all my years of critiquing mainstream economics, I've never read anything quite as delusional as the work of Nordhaus and his colleagues on the economics of climate change.'[56] Keen has no doubts whatsoever that we need to halt the use of fossil fuels as quickly as possible or we will face a total catastrophe. He also feels that we should abandon the whole COP process and adopt a 'Tradeable Universal Carbon Credits' scheme in its place. Keen is, however, not very hopeful of implementing this scheme under present circumstances.

We need to halt the use of fossil fuels as quickly as possible or we will face a total catastrophe

We have seen that there are now at least some economists who are taking the environmental crisis seriously, and are contributing to the growing discipline of environmental economics. We will end this chapter on a positive note by considering the work of *Kate Raworth.* She is Senior Associate at Oxford University's Environmental Change Institute and the instigator of (what she has called) 'Doughnut Economics.'[57]

Doughnut Economics

How does Doughnut Economics work? In her doughnut, Raworth places the nine planetary boundaries around the outside edge. As we have seen, we are already over the limits of six of these boundaries, and this threatens our survival and that of much of the world's biodiversity. Raworth places 12 social dimensions that are derived from the SDGs on the doughnut's inner edge: food; health; education; income and work; water and sanitation; energy; networks; housing; gender equality; social equity; political voice; and peace and justice. No person should fall beneath these inner boundaries. According to Raworth we need to find the sweet spot within the doughnut that is both ecologically safe (not transgressing the planetary boundaries) and socially just (not falling through the inner social boundaries) for humanity.

Raworth considers that we need to change the goal from GDP and endless economic growth to thriving in balance, attaining the sweet spot in the doughnut. The environment and its components (*eg* pollution) should no longer be seen as an externality in Raworth's model, but included within a new economic model that is regenerative by design.

Doughnut Economics can seem like a utopian ideal that would never to put into practice, but the Dutch city of Amsterdam has proved that idea wrong.[58] The Municipality of Amsterdam authorized the Amsterdam Circular 2020–2025 strategy in April 2020. This had an initial two-year practical action plan, but the aim is for Amsterdam to have a completely circular economy by 2050.[59] In this scheme materials and products will be used and reused nearly continually, preventing waste and pollution. The city aims to live within planetary boundaries, while keeping the social foundation in mind. The ambitious plan seeks to decrease greenhouse gas emissions, safeguard biodiversity, increase the quality of the living environment for people, and to use renewable raw materials, such as wood or flax. Amsterdam will no longer be dependent on non-renewable raw materials. Value chains examine the complete life cycle of a product or process. Amsterdam determined the most important value chains it can influence, these being: food and organic waste streams; consumer goods; and the built environment. A number of other cities around the world are beginning to follow Amsterdam's example: Copenhagen, Brussels, Dunedin in New Zealand, Glasgow and Portland, Oregon.

In the final chapter of *Doughnut Economics* we read: 'Once we accept the economy's inherent complexity, we can shape its ever-evolving dynamics through smart stewardship. That opens up the possibility of turning today's divisive and degenerative economies into ones that are distributive and regenerative by design. And it invites us to become agnostic about growth, creating economies that enable us to thrive, whether or not they are growing.'[60] It is notable that Raworth uses the word 'stewardship,' a much debated concept in theological circles in recent years. We will turn to that next.

5 The Stewardship Ethic Revisited

> No generation has a freehold on this earth. All we have is a life tenancy with a full repairing lease. (Baroness [Margaret] Thatcher)[61]

Is the stewardship ethic outmoded or is it the best pragmatic option for working in the real world? Stewardship used to be the go-to ethic whenever the environment was mentioned. Bishops, professors and politicians would use the word to signal how we should respond to the need to care for the natural world. This has now changed. The stewardship ethic has been challenged at academic level for years and many Christians, who are active on environment, are now aware of this. But, while some Christians have been moving away from the concept, others, including secular organizations, politicians, scientists and wider church members have been taking up the idea. There is even now a journal called *Earth Stewardship*.[62] What has been happening, and is it aiding or hindering an effective response to the environmental crisis?[63]

What is the Stewardship Ethic?

The starting point for the stewardship ethic is found in the first two chapters of Genesis. The term 'dominion' or 'rule' has a long history of interpretation and challenge (Gen 1.28). The three-way combination of humans as creatures, made in God's image and commanded to rule, provides a foundation for stewardship thinking. The Christian Assisi Declaration explained that, 'It is especially through man and woman, made in the image and likeness of God and entrusted with a unique dominion over all visible creatures, that the Lord's goodness and providence are to be manifested.' The declaration described dominion as 'a stewardship in symbiosis with all creatures.'[64]

Genesis 2.15 contains the command to work (serve) and protect the Garden of Eden. It combines ecocentric ethics, which consider the good of nature as a whole, with anthropocentric ethics, which look to the needs of humanity. It also draws on theocentric ethics and the desire to honour God in our treatment of the earth. If the biblical concept of stewardship begins with tending the Garden of Eden, it progresses by drawing on agricultural situations such as in Lev 19.9–10 and 25.1–7. It is essentially a management ethic of nature to provide for human cultivation while enabling sustainability for the rest of life and for future generations.

In the Book of Isaiah, space is given for wilderness where wild animals roam freely. Mountains and deserts are seen as divine dwelling places where humans encounter God, but everyday life is lived out in a farmed context, even in the eschatological future.[65] Stewardship is far from being the only biblical environmental ethic. It is mainly derived from Old Testament teaching, with some resonances in New Testament parables. Calvin B DeWitt introduced the concept of earth-keeping in understanding stewardship: 'As the Lord keeps and sustains us, so must we keep and sustain our Lord's creation.'[66] He combined this with a sabbath principle ('We must provide for creation's sabbath rests'), and a fruitfulness principle, ('We should enjoy, but must not destroy, creation's fruitfulness'). In considering stewardship, the role of management, value and relationships are key factors.

Stewardship is frequently used as an ethic in the secular world. For example, in considering the role of the state in public health, Lord (John) Krebs advocated the stewardship model which 'recognizes that the state ...has a responsibility to provide the conditions under which people can lead healthy lives.'[67] Krebs proposed an intervention ladder, ranging from simply monitoring or giving information at the bottom levels, to offering incentives in the middle, to restricting or eliminating choice at the highest intervention levels. This ladder is currently being played out in UK traffic situations with measures from lower to higher being: no tax on electric cars (an incentive); ULEZ zones (a cost); LTNs (restrictions on traffic); to a future ban on new fossil-fuel cars.[68] These measures will reduce carbon emissions and other pollutants and the principles could be fruitfully applied to other areas as we transition toward a green economy.

Stewardship is frequently used as an ethic in the secular world

Critiques of Stewardship

Among the many theological critiques of stewardship, four have particular resonance. The first critique responds to the complexity of the earth's systems and our conceit in believing that we can ever understand the subtle functioning of our planetary system enough to manage it. Both James Lovelock and Clare Palmer raise this difficulty and the danger of human arrogance toward nature to believe that we are in control.[69] The second criticism concerns the relationship between humans and God. Stewardship is flawed, if God is seen as an absentee landlord, with humans left with the earth to look after it. This draws on the Parable of the Talents in Matt 25.14–30, where the owner goes away, entrusting his property to his servants. The third concern relates to the relative status of humans and the rest of creation. Here, stewardship might be seen as implying a hierarchy, with humans above the rest of creation and thereby separate from it. The final critique concerns our relationship with the rest of creation. Stewardship implies nature needs us. This stems from a Renaissance idea that God created nature unfinished, and it is the role of humans to perfect nature. With all these critiques, one needs to ask if they are fundamental flaws in the concept of stewardship, or flaws in the way stewardship has been interpreted and presented? If stewardship is to be re-assessed in response to these concerns, it needs to nurture a strong sense of the immanence of God, a very humble sense of humanity as part of creation and a self-effacing approach to our role as creatures bearing God's image.

Christological Approaches

One further concern is that the concept of stewardship does not obviously connect to New Testament theology *per se*. How can we make these connections? Placing Christ at the heart of Christian environmental ethics opens incarnational, redemptive and eschatological pathways. Rowan Williams explores some of these implications, explaining that since Christ is fully present, Christians, as his body, are fully 'in earth' where God is bringing life through Christ.[70] The incarnation of Christ is set out in the context of creation in John 1: Susan Miller highlights the word 'flesh' (*sarx*) as an attribute of all creatures and not simply humans.[71] Christ fully joined the creative order and therefore his followers should be active in caring for his creation. Similarly, the bodily resurrection of Christ hallows the material world and can be a powerful motivator to care for it. An understanding of the cosmic role of Christ in Col 1.15–20, has been used as a basis for an understanding of the redemptive power of Christ's sacrifice for the whole of creation as well as the role of Christ's followers, as his body, in holding (caring for) creation with him.[72] Finally, with an increasing eschatological emphasis on the renewal rather than a replacement of creation, motivation for environmental action can be derived from the future destiny of the earth, rather than purely from our responsibility given at creation.[73]

Beyond these concepts, there are several approaches using virtues ethics, including wisdom, hope, lament and simplicity. A model of humans as priests of creation comes from the Eastern church and others put an emphasis on eco justice.[74]

Christological Approaches in Practice

The huge strength of these approaches for a Christian approach to the environment is very simply the focus on Christ. All are drawn from the New Testament and deepen a specifically Christian understanding of our relationship with the rest of creation and responsibility to care for it. They enable Christians to integrate care for creation within an understanding of the gospel. This means that there is a natural pathway to understanding creation care as missional action. Their spiritual depth will resonate with committed Christians and especially those with a firm grasp of the New Testament texts. They are motivational and help those who have a love for Christ and a love for nature, to understand how they connect.

The challenge of these approaches is that they can be complex as an initial introduction to the practical need to care for creation, especially for Christians with a less comprehensive understanding of the New Testament. This can be overcome with teaching, leading to an enhancement of understanding of the Christian faith overall. A bigger challenge is that they are not as useful for a shared motivational ethic when working or volunteering in partnership with secular people and organizations, and those with environmental concerns who are members of other faiths. How can we be authentic as Christians with a Christocentric motivational driver for our environmental action, while also working with shared values and motivations in a mixed society? In effect, how can we be both light and salt? Would a nuanced understanding of stewardship in combination with Christological approaches, provide a broader basis for our understanding and action?

A Community of Creation

Richard Bauckham sets out some shortcomings of the stewardship ethic but does not entirely reject it.[75] He seeks to set it within the wider context of the biblical narrative and proposes that we understand our role as being part of a 'community of creation,' where humans find a leadership role from within the community of creation rather than ruling over it. He places this within a Christological framework, drawing on Rom 8.18–23 and Revelation 21–22 to point towards an ultimate renewal of creation and the role of Christians as we live out our lives in the light of this. Here stewardship, in Genesis 1 and 2, is a starting point on which to build a deeper understanding that is holistic and engages with Christocentric viewpoints. Following this community of creation approach enables Christians to be motivated through their Christian faith towards environmental action, while being able to have a shared understanding of creation care with those outside the Christian community. Bauckham's views are biocentric with a strong emphasis on intrinsic value. In reassessing stewardship, is it possible to combine an understanding of intrinsic value with those secular management models, such as TEEB, which use extrinsic and instrumental value?

Human leadership from within the community of creation rather than ruling over it

Environmental Pragmatism

A secular approach that has been successful in climate negotiations is 'environmental pragmatism.' This tends towards consequentialism and takes a flexible approach to value and ethical starting points. Environmental pragmatists are focused on outcomes that give the most positive result for the environment and for humanity, present and future. They argue that anthropocentric rationales for environmental protection are often more persuasive, and this means that they are likely to be more effective in protecting the environment.[76] Environmental pragmatists, such as Steven Fesmire, tend to be critical of supporters of theoretical and idealistic environmental ethics, who advocate for a complete change of society, arguing that this is unrealistic. Instead, Fesmire follows John Dewey's distinction between a continuously planning society and a planned society, arguing that the former is more robust because of the way that it can develop in response to circumstances.[77] Fesmire disliked the top-down climate ethics of the Kyoto Protocol, which he considered punitive. He contrasted these with the pledge and review bottom-up approach of the Paris Agreement, which was aided by the thinking of Andrew Light, a pragmatist philosopher and US Assistant Secretary of Energy for International Affairs. In responding to climate change, Light does not see an emphasis on obligations as helpful, but advocates an approach that focuses on the opportunities created by responding to the crisis and the benefits this can bring to individuals and society, by building better communities and institutions.[78] This is highly anthropocentric but is likely to be more successful in democratic societies, and mirrors Mark Carney's views (above).

One danger with environmental pragmatism is that the concept of intrinsic value can be marginalized. This could mean that its early successes might eventually lead to failure and environmental breakdown. Pragmatism is a powerful tool in achieving the possible. However, a practical ethic that is less anthropocentric is needed if we are to respond effectively to the climate and ecological crisis in the long term, as the 2005 Millennium Ecosystem Assessment warned. How might stewardship be developed to be both pragmatic and theologically robust? We will consider this in our final chapter.

6

Being Earth-keepers as God and the Earth Keeps Us

> Finally, beloved, whatever is true, whatever is honourable, whatever is just, whatever is pure, whatever is pleasing, whatever is commendable, if there is any excellence and if there is anything worthy of praise, think about these things. (Phil 4.8 NRSV)

Starting with Value

One approach that is both pragmatic and begins with a strong sense of value is 'appreciative inquiry' (AI). Rather than being problem focused, AI seeks to build on strengths following a pattern that can be described as: discover, dream, design, and deliver.

As a case-study, Yuliani *et al* sought to use AI in developing community-based conservation in Indonesia.[79] Whereas a problem-solving approach tended to undermine confidence in local knowledge, AI built self-confidence and enabled conservation that, in valuing indigenous community and natural habitats, enabled both to flourish. Jule and Castellon used AI to explore environmental education in Canadian Christian schools.[80] They partnered AI with stewardship, finding a biblical basis in Phil 4.8, which wove in an understanding of intrinsic value. They discovered that this approach led to holistic development of environmental education and practice. This leads full circle back to the concept of the community of creation, where humans lead humbly from within creation, seeking what can be celebrated and enabling ecological flourishing. Like ecology, care for the environment is multifaceted, demanding a range of approaches.

Stewardship Revisited and Revised

Stewardship has many shortcomings but it continues to make an effective starting point for environmental action at all levels. It becomes a blind alley if it is seen as a destination and the only approach to environmental action. If it is seen more as a gateway leading to more holistic approaches, both Christian and secular, it can have a dynamic role for Christians as they take up environmental concern. It also enables a point of partnership with secular people and organizations as well as those of other faiths.

Christocentric and other alternative Christian environmental ethics to stewardship are highly valuable in helping Christians understand more deeply the theological connections between God, people and the rest of creation. They are also effective as practical ethics for environmental projects run within Christian contexts. Given that environmental projects are often situations where Christians are collaborating with other bodies and worldviews, they are less user friendly in these situations of plurality. The stewardship ethic, however, is widely understood and indeed forms the basis for many secular responses to the environmental crisis.

Rather than discard the stewardship ethic for its flaws, we would advocate using it for its strengths in partnership with other approaches. Environmental pragmatism is a dominant approach in the secular world and AI shows the potential for combining stewardship with a modern secular approach and drawing in a biblical virtues ethic in the process.

Interrelational Stewardship

If stewardship is too useful a tool in our kit-bag to discard, how might we develop it? We close by proposing the concept of interrelational stewardship:

Interrelational with God: emphasizing the immanence of God and our relationship with and continued dependency on him as we seek to be disciples at a time of environmental crisis.

Interrelational with creation: understanding that we are fellow creatures within creation and our decisions and actions need to be always made in that context and for the benefit of all.

Interrelational with other faiths: realizing our shared values in the care for the planet and building on our common goals.

Interrelational with the secular world: recognizing the importance of global agencies and initiatives, plus secular ideas from science, economics and other sources; seeking to work in partnership at all levels from international to local communities.

Interrelational with theology: not stopping at stewardship but deepening our understanding through Christological approaches to creation care.

Interrelational with mission: seeing environmental stewardship as an essential strand of mission that complements rather than distracts from Christian mission as proclamation, discipleship, responding to human need, and seeking justice for all.

Conclusion

Interrelational stewardship is a fruitful tool for Christians as we seek to work alongside so many others in responding to the environmental crisis that is fast engulfing us. It is a powerful discipleship tool as we engage with Christians and churches ever more widely in our calling as disciples in the complex world of the twenty-first century. Let us not reject stewardship, but work humbly to deepen our understanding of how we can be earth-keepers as God and the earth keeps us.

Notes

1 J Rockström *et al*, 'A safe operating space for humanity,' *Nature* 461, 2009, pp 472–475: https://doi.org/10.1038/461472a
2 W Steffen *et al*, 'Planetary boundaries: Guiding human development on a changing planet,' *Science* 347, 2015, 1259855: https://doi.org/10.1126/science.1259855
3 K Richardson *et al*, 'Earth beyond six of nine planetary boundaries,' *Science Advances* 9, 2023, eadh2458: https://doi.org/10.1126/sciadv.adh2458
4 For more background on this concept see: E E Ellis, *Anthropocene: A Very Short Introduction* (Oxford University Press, 2018); T Howles, *Responding Faithfully to the Environmental Crisis: Christianity at the Time of the Anthropocene* (Grove Ethics booklet E 192).
5 D Carrington, 'Geologists reject declaration of Anthropocene epoch,' *The Guardian* (22 March 2024): https://www.theguardian.com/science/2024/mar/22/geologists-reject-declaration-of-anthropocene-epoch (accessed 10 June 2024).
6 *National Geographic*, 'Preservation,' encyclopaedic entry: https://education.nationalgeographic.org/resource/preservation/ (accessed 11 June 2024).
7 M J Hodson and M R Hodson, *An Introduction to Environmental Ethics* (Grove Ethics booklet E 184).
8 R Attfield, *Environmental Thought: A Short History* (Cambridge: Polity, 2021) pp 91–95.
9 Q Luthy, 'How Conservation Contributes to the Displacement of Indigenous People,' *EARTH.ORG* (8 March 2023): https://earth.org/conservation-indigenous-people/ (accessed 11 June 2024).
10 M S Fletcher, R Hamilton, W Dressler and L Palmer, 'Indigenous knowledge and the shackles of wilderness,' *Proceedings of the National Academy of Sciences, USA*, 118, 2021, e2022218118.
11 H Briggs and V Gill, 'Biodiversity: Can we set aside a third of our planet for nature?' *BBC News* (14 December 2022): https://www.bbc.co.uk/news/science-environment-63955526 (accessed 12 June 2024).
12 G P Marsh, *Man and Nature: Or, Physical Geography as Modified by Human Action* (New York: C Scribner, 1864) p 36.
13 A Leopold, *A Sand County Almanac* (Oxford University Press, 1949).
14 For a more detailed account of Leopold's thinking see Attfield, *Environmental Thought, op cit,* pp 125–135.
15 R Carson, *Silent Spring* (Boston, MA: Houghton Mifflin, 1962).
16 For an assessment of all these publications and more see Attfield, *Environmental Thought, op cit,* chapter 7, pp 141–163.
17 Report of the World Commission on Environment and Development: Our Common Future (Oxford University Press, 1987): https://sustainabledevelopment.un.org/content/documents/5987our-common-future.pdf (accessed 13 June 2024).

18 Statement by M F Strong, Secretary-General United Nations Conference on Environment and Development, at the opening of the United Nations Conference on Environment and Development, Rio de Janeiro, Brazil, 3 June 1992. See: https://www.mauricestrong.net/index.php?option=com_content&view=article&id=165&Itemid=86 (accessed 29 June 2024).
19 United Nations Conference on Environment and Development, Rio de Janeiro, Brazil (3–14 June 1992): https://www.un.org/en/conferences/environment/rio1992 (accessed 29 June 2024).
20 Rio Declaration on Environment and Development (3–14 June 1992): https://www.un.org/en/development/desa/population/migration/generalassembly/docs/globalcompact/A_CONF.151_26_Vol.I_Declaration.pdf (accessed 29 June 2024).
21 See: R Therivel and G Wood, *Methods of Environmental and Social Impact Assessment* (New York and London: Routledge, 2018, fourth edition).
22 Agenda 21. United Nations Conference on Environment and Development, Rio de Janeiro, Brazil (3–14 June 1992). https://sustainabledevelopment.un.org/content/documents/Agenda21.pdf (accessed 1 July 2024).
23 Convention on Long-range Transboundary Air Pollution: https://unece.org/sites/default/files/2021-05/1979%20CLRTAP.e.pdf (accessed 1 July 2024).
24 United Nations Environment Programme: The Montreal Protocol on Substances that Deplete the Ozone Layer: https://ozone.unep.org/treaties/montreal-protocol-substances-deplete-ozone-layer/text (accessed 1 July 2024).
25 The Intergovernmental Panel on Climate Change (IPCC): https://www.ipcc.ch/ (accessed 2 July 2024).
26 IPCC: Climate Change 2021: The Physical Science Basis: https://www.ipcc.ch/report/sixth-assessment-report-working-group-i/ (accessed 2 July 2024).
27 The United Nations Framework Convention on Climate Change (UNFCCC): https://unfccc.int/ (accessed 2 July 2024).
28 The United Nations Framework Convention on Climate Change (UNFCCC): Article 3. Principles. https://unfccc.int/resource/ccsites/zimbab/conven/text/art03.htm (accessed 2 July 2024).
29 For more on this and climate scepticism see M J Hodson and M R Hodson, *The Ethics of Climatic Scepticism* (Grove Ethics booklet E177).
30 G W Bush, 'Text of a Letter from the President to Senators Hagel, Helms, Craig, and Roberts,' *The White House* (13 March 2001) https://georgewbush-whitehouse.archives.gov/news/releases/2001/03/20010314.html (accessed 2 July 2024).
31 See: United Nations, The Paris Agreement: https://unfccc.int/process-and-meetings/the-paris-agreement (accessed 2 July 2024).
32 United Nations. 'COP27 ends with announcement of historic loss and damage fund' (22 November 2022): https://www.unep.org/news-and-stories/story/cop27-ends-announcement-historic-loss-and-damage-fund (accessed 2 July 2024).
33 For more information on both CDR and SRM see: IPCC, Climate Change 2022. Mitigation of Climate Change. Working Group III contribution to the Sixth Assessment Report of the Intergovernmental Panel on Climate Change: https://www.ipcc.ch/report/ar6/wg3/downloads/report/IPCC_AR6_WGIII_FullReport.pdf (accessed 6 July 2024).
34 C J Preston, 'Ethics and geoengineering: reviewing the moral issues raised by solar radiation management and carbon dioxide removal,' *WIREs Climate Change* 4, 2013, pp 23–37: https://doi.org/10.1002/wcc.198
35 The Convention on Biological Diversity: https://www.cbd.int/convention (accessed 2 July 2024).
36 Millennium Ecosystem Assessment (2005): https://www.millenniumassessment.org/en/index.html (accessed 6 July 2024).

37 Millennium Ecosystem Assessment, *Ecosystems and Human Well-being: Synthesis* (Washington, DC: Island Press, 2005) p 58: https://www.millennium assessment.org/documents/document.356.aspx.pdf (accessed 6 July 2024).
38 WWF Living Planet Report 2022: https://www.wwf.org.uk/our-reports/living-planet-report-2022 (accessed 6 July 2024).
39 United Nations, Millennium Development Goals: https://www.un.org/millennium goals/ (accessed 6 July 2024).
40 United Nations Department of Economic and Social Affairs, Sustainable Development Goals: https://sdgs.un.org/goals (accessed 6 July 2024).
41 United Nations, 'Progress towards the Sustainable Development Goals,' Report of the Secretary-General. General Assembly Economic and Social Council 2024 session: https://unstats.un.org/sdgs/files/report/2024/SG-SDG-Progress-Report-2024-advanced-unedited-version.pdf (accessed 6 July 2024).
42 For details on HS2 and ancient woodland see: P Barkham, '"It's an enormous act of ecological vandalism": the ancient forests under threat from HS2' *The Guardian* (6 October 2019): https://www.theguardian.com/environment/2019/oct/06/its-an-enormous-act-of-ecological-vandalism-the-ancient-forests-under-threat-from-hs2 (accessed 2 July 2024); Woodland Trust, HS2 Rail Link: https://www.woodlandtrust.org.uk/protecting-trees-and-woods/campaign-with-us/hs2-rail-link/ (accessed 2 July 2024).
43 S Keen, 'The Economics of COPOUT28,' *Resilience* (5 January 2024): https://www.resilience.org/stories/2024-01-05/the-economics-of-copout28/ (accessed 8 July 2024).
44 S Smith, *Environmental Economics. A Very Short Introduction* (Oxford University Press) p 11.
45 C Hepburn and A Bowen, 'Prosperity with growth: economic growth, climate change and environmental limits' in R Fouquet (ed), *Handbook on Energy and Climate Change* (Cheltenham: Edward Elgar Publishing, 2013) pp 617–638.
46 D H Meadows, D L Meadows, J Randers, W Behrens III, *The Limits to Growth* (Falls Church, VA: Potomac Associates–Universe Books, 1972).
47 D Weisbach and C R Sunstein, 'Climate Change and Discounting the Future: A Guide for the Perplexed,' *Yale Law and Policy Review* 27, 2009, pp 433–457.
48 Leopold, *A Sand County Almanac, op cit.*
49 T Juniper, *What has Nature Ever Done for Us?* (London: Profile Books, 2013).
50 The Economics of Ecosystems and Biodiversity (TEEB): https://teebweb.org/about/approach/ (accessed 29 July 2024).
51 R Bauckham, *Living with Other Creatures* (Waco, TX: Baylor University Press, 2011) p 232.
52 For a helpful explanation of 'cap and trade' and 'carbon pricing' see K Hayhoe, *Saving Us* (New York: One Signal, 2021) pp 156–160.
53 M Carney, 'Lecture 4: From Climate Crisis to Real Prosperity,' The Reith Lectures 2020: How We Get What We Value (23 December 2020 at 9am, BBC Radio 4): https://downloads.bbc.co.uk/radio4/reith2020/Reith_2020_Lecture_4_transcript_V2.pdf (accessed 9 July 2024).
54 P Dasgupta, *The Economics of Biodiversity: The Dasgupta Review* (London: H M Treasury, 2021): https://assets.publishing.service.gov.uk/government/uploads/system/uploads/attachment_data/file/962785/The_Economics_of_Biodiversity_The_Dasgupta_Review_Full_Report.pdf (accessed 9 July 2024).
55 The Economics of Climate Change: The Stern Review. London School of Economics and Political Science: https://www.lse.ac.uk/granthaminstitute/publication/the-economics-of-climate-change-the-stern-review/ (accessed 9 July 2024).
56 'The Economics of COPOUT28,' *op cit.*
57 See K Raworth, *Doughnut Economics* (New York: Random House Business, 2018).

58 M-C Florian, 'How Amsterdam Uses the Doughnut Economics Model to Create a Balanced Strategy for Both the People and the Environment,' *ArchDaily* (26 April 2024): https://www.archdaily.com/997291/how-amsterdam-uses-the-doughnut-economics-model-to-create-a-balanced-strategy-for-both-the-people-and-the-environment (accessed 10 July 2024).
59 City of Amsterdam, 'Implementation Agenda for a Circular Amsterdam 2023–2026': https://assets.amsterdam.nl/publish/pages/1043702/implementation-agenda-circular.pdf (accessed 10 July 2024).
60 Raworth, *Doughnut Economics, op cit,* p 286.
61 Margaret Thatcher, Speech to Conservative Party Conference, 14 October 1988.
62 *Earth Stewardship*, Wiley online journals: https://esajournals.onlinelibrary.wiley.com/journal/28353617 (accessed 10 July 2024).
63 For a detailed exploration of the debate on the stewardship ethic see R J Berry (ed), *Environmental Stewardship* (London: T and T Clark, 2006).
64 Alliance of Religions and Conservation, *The Assisi Declarations* (Bath: ARC, 1986).
65 M R Hodson, *Uncovering Isaiah's Environmental Ethics* (Grove Ethics booklet E 161).
66 CB DeWitt, Three Biblical Principles For Environmental Stewardship: http://www.leaderu.com/theology/environment.html (accessed 8 July 2024).
67 J Krebs, *Public Health Ethical Issues* (London: Nuffield Council on Bioethics, 2007) p v.
68 ULEZ are Ultra Low Emission Zones and LTNs are Low Traffic Neighbourhoods.
69 J Lovelock, 'The Fallible Concept of Stewardship of the Earth' and C Palmer, 'Stewardship: A Case Study in Environmental Ethics,' in R J Berry, *Environmental Stewardship, op cit,* pp 106–111, and pp 63–75.
70 R Williams, *Christ the Heart of Creation* (London: Bloomsbury Continuum, 2018).
71 S Miller, 'John's Gospel' in H Marlow and M Harris (eds), *The Oxford Handbook of the Bible and Ecology* (Oxford University Press, 2022) p 231.
72 M J Hodson and M R Hodson, *Climate Change, Faith and Rural Communities* (Northampton: ATP, 2011).
73 See, for example, N T Wright, *Surprised by Hope* (London: SPCK, 2007) p 240.
74 A summary of these can be found in M Hodson and M Hodson, *Climate Change, Faith and Rural Communities*, *op cit,* pp 18–20.
75 R Bauckham, *Bible and Ecology* (London: Darton, Longman and Todd, 2010).
76 C Palmer, K McShane and R Sandler, 'Environmental Ethics,' *Annual Review of Environment and Resources* 39, 2014, pp 433–434.
77 S Fesmire, 'Environmental Pragmatism,' in H LaFollette (ed), *International Encyclopedia of Ethics* (Hoboken, NJ: Wiley, 2022): https://philarchive.org/rec/FESEP (accessed 30 July 2024).
78 J Donhauser, Andrew Light and the Paris Agreement (London, Ontario: Rotman Institute of Philosophy): https://www.rotman.uwo.ca/andrew-light-and-the-paris-agreement/ (accessed 2 July 2024).
79 E L Yuliani, H Adnan, C J Pierce Colfer and Y Indriatmoko, 'Problem-solving *versus* appreciative inquiry approaches in community-based conservation,' *Forests, Trees and Livelihoods*, 2014, 24(2), pp 97–111.
80 A Jule and AR Castellon, 'The Grace to Grow Deeper: A Case Study of Environmentalism in a Canadian Christian School,' *International Christian Community of Teacher Educators Journal, George Fox University*, 15, 2020: https://digitalcommons.georgefox.edu/icctej/vol15/iss2/2/ (accessed 30 July 2024).